The Easy Way to Invest:

Start Small, Get Rich
Investing with Small Amounts

Susan Calhoun

The Easy Way to Invest:

Start Small, Get Rich Investing With Small
Amounts

Susan Calhoun

Table of Contents

Contents

Introduction

When money is tight, it's hard to believe you have any extra cash to invest for your future. Today, many people spend every cent they earn, with little to show for it after all the bills are paid. Investment gurus tell us to put 5% or 10% percent of our income aside, but for anyone living paycheck to paycheck, that's a huge amount of money to spare. Still - don't you feel like you're missing the bus if you don't invest *something* for your future? We all know that our financial health depends on the saving and investing habits we make part of our lives. This book shows how you can change your habits to start building wealth with small amounts of $5, $10 or $25. Getting started even with just a few bucks at a time can lead to tens or hundreds of thousands of dollars in your future investment account!

Investing with small amounts gets you into the investing game with cash you can spare out of your everyday expenses. You don't have to "do without" or eat rice and beans for years to find money to start investing! While you may not build extreme wealth with just a few dollars (even though it has been done!), you'll take the habit of investing you learn here plus other investing skills you need to build great wealth. Investing small amounts also means you can get started putting away some cash without worrying about first paying off all your debt. Using small amounts to invest, there's no reason to wait until sometime in the future. You can start right now to put money away, in investments with low risk and good returns. This book will show you how to find the extra money and where to invest it, a little at a time.

Small-dollar investing comes with a wonderful long-term payoff. You begin to build your personal net worth and accumulate wealth for yourself and your family. Let's say you start by putting $5 per week into an account that pays 5% interest. Five bucks is such a small amount, you probably spend that each week without even realizing it's gone. In five years, you'll have more than $1,500 saved up.

That's $1,500 that could have just gone out the window. Instead, that cash cushion will be there when you need a new appliance or want a family vacation. If you increase that weekly investment to $10 a week, you'll have over $3,000. That might not sound like much on the surface, but isn't it better to have three grand instead of zero at the end of those five years? The idea isn't that investing five or ten bucks will make you rich - instead, the secret of getting rich is in the method.

You're not trying to get super rich on five bucks a week. You're starting the habit of saving and investing. As you start the ball rolling, you can increase your contributions and at the same time learn how to exceed 5% returns. Soon, you'll find your portfolio is expanding beyond anything you ever expected! As you go through this book, you'll discover ways to find extra money to invest, as well as how to search for better returns on your investments. All this will help grow your investment portfolio even faster. Remember, the important thing is to just get started and make a commitment saving and investing.

The beauty of investing is that anyone can do it, whether you have a lot of money or just a little. You might hear that it's only the high rollers that succeed in the market. Consider Warren Buffet, who started at age 11 with just three shares of stock! He is just one example of how starting small can lead to big portfolios. It's not about means; it's about your mindset: saving, investing and continuing to learn is the key. Investing is active, not passive - you have to take specific action in order to invest in yourself and your future.

Successful investors need the same skills whether they are investing $5 or $5,000,000. For starters, you have to focus on how your money can work for you, rather than the other way around. Continually ask yourself: Is there an investment that meets my financial goals, and which pays a better return?

Later chapters will explain how to calculate the best returns on your money. For now, simply focus on finding affordable investments so that your money works for you at the lowest cost. That's the purpose of this book - to show you how to invest the most money at the lowest possible cost and highest return. After that, it's all about continuing to add investments to your portfolio and watching it grow.

Chapter 1: Three Easy Steps to Build Wealth with Small Amounts

There are just three basic steps to start investing if you're working with small amounts of money. First, you'll find the extra cash and put it aside at least weekly. Next, you'll set up an account where you can stash it and build your balances. Third, you'll move the money into investments of your choosing. That's really all there is to it! Sounds simple, and it is, but it's not easy. Finding money and not spending it can be a challenge. And once you've invested it, you have to learn to invest wisely and keep your costs down.

The three steps are:

Step One: Decide to deposit money at least weekly, in whatever amount works for you. You really do have the money to start, even if you feel broke. Try this: Right now, go to your wallet. Pull out every single dollar bill you have in your wallet, and put that in a jar where you'll start collecting your deposit cash. No bills in your wallet? Take the change in your wallet, around the house, or in your car, and put that in the jar instead. Put your loose bills and change in the jar at the end of each day, and on Saturday open up an account and deposit it. Even if you only have $2, it's a start.

If you don't have loose change around, start snooping around your garage, attic, basement or that closet where you store things. Pull out any good condition items you haven't used in a while, and head over to Craigslist and list them for sale. You can make instant cash for things lying around the house you don't need. Or, if you have an eBay and PayPal account, list items for sale there. If you often buy your lunch, take lunch to work and put the $5-$10 you saved into the jar. Here are some more simple ways to save a few bucks starting this week:

* Skip the manicure this week.

* Hold a garage sale this weekend.

* Cook at home instead of eating out this week.

* Don't get coffee to go, put the $$ in your jar.

* Rent a movie at the library instead of going to the theater or buying pay-per-view.

You get the idea. For instant results, search for a way to have some extra money right away that you can get started with. While this book uses $5 a week as a guideline, you can make it as much or as little as you like. Remember - the more you can put away, the faster you'll see results! Everyone can find money to invest.

Step Two: Set up a "base account". This is a bank account where you'll deposit your investing cash - the loose change or garage sale earnings. You'll use this account to accumulate funds. Once your balances start to grow, you'll transfer funds from this account into an investment account and any other investing vehicles that you choose. (See Chapter 2 for more on your base account.)

Step Three: Now start investing your money! Once you have enough funds in your base account, you can start to invest. While reading this book, you'll examine different options depending on how much you have to invest, and choose the right one to get started. The more you save up in your base account, the more investment funds you'll have to work with. Your money goes to work in your chosen investment vehicle, providing returns and dividends as well as passive income.

That's the three-step plan, pure and simple. The rest of this book will explore each step and give you more ideas for investments that don't require a huge amount of up-front cash but still provide a solid return.

For now, in order to invest, you need funds. Make a commitment to yourself to put aside an amount of cash each week. There are still many institutions that will allow you to open a base account with little or no money. Once you have some cash, look for an account to open as described in Chapter 2 below.

There's one more thing you need to know before you begin: the right questions to ask about your money and your investments. There are two questions investors ask before they buy an investment:

1. Is this the best use of my money?

2. Am I getting the best return I can for this investment?

Add a third for the beginning investor: How can I save more money to put to work investing?

Those questions will make you a lot of money. Contrary to what the average investor has been told for years, you do not want to put your money into a "buy and hold" investment indefinitely, never to be touched. This method wastes serious time, and in investing, time is money. Instead, learn to regularly review your portfolio, and make sure your investments are working as hard as they can. Doing anything else is a recipe for losing money.

As you review the information in this book about where to invest, you should always ask whether you could make a better return on investment with a different investment vehicle. For example, if you plan to put your money in a savings account that pays a half percent (.05%) interest, would you be better off paying down a credit card with an interest rate of 27.9%?

Take another example. When you consider putting your money into a money market fund, ask whether the rate of interest is better than the rate you could get from a bond purchase. It's true that investing in something safe usually means you'll earn a lower interest rate. But in today's climate, where prices are rising, is it truly safe to keep your money invested at .05% when inflation may reach 2% or 3% in the next year? Asking the right questions will help you discover your options and put your money to work, no matter how small the amount. You'll learn more about how to analyze your investments in the coming chapters.

With that information in hand, it's time to open your base investing accounts.

Chapter 2: Open a Base Account

The first step toward building your portfolio of investments and personal wealth is to open a new account for stashing your cash. Call it your "base account", since as you add money to this cash account it will form the base of your investment portfolio. This account will also be connected to an investment account at a discount brokerage. You can then easily transfer money from this base account into your respective investment accounts.

Make sure that this account isn't linked to your everyday bill paying and spending accounts, otherwise your hard-earned cash could be gone in a hurry. Don't leave yourself open to temptation to spend this money before you invest it. Instead, consider opening a new bank account with an online bank, or a separate savings account at a different bank or credit union from the one you usually use.

You can open either a checking or a savings account, but you won't need checks or a debit card for this account. If you open a savings account, be aware that federal regulations restrict you from making more than three withdrawals per month from savings accounts, or you'll risk having the account closed. Many banks now require at least $100 to open an account, so if you absolutely cannot find a bank account without this minimum, stick to your coin jar until you reach $100.

The good news is, this account doesn't need any bells and whistles. Instead, it's just important to keep your costs low, preferably at zero. The perfect base account comes with four things:

1. No minimum balance requirement, or a only a small deposit required to open the account

2. No monthly maintenance or other fees

3. The ability to check your balance online

4. A small rate of interest to help you along

As noted above, don't bother ordering checks or a debit card, since you won't need them and you want to reduce the temptation to withdraw and spend. You can use the initial set of checks if you need to withdraw money, but for the most part, withdrawals from this account will all be electronic transfers into your investment accounts. All you'll really need is the routing number or ABA number of the bank and the account number of your new account. You can easily get the bank routing number from your bank's customer service representatives.

Another great option for a base account is a checking account with a brokerage. This way you can keep your saved cash and investments all together. Several discount brokers now offer interest checking accounts that can be linked to a brokerage account. There are usually no or low initial deposit requirements, but be sure to confirm current prices and also make sure there are no maintenance fees! If this option appeals to you, check out these reputable banks and their account:

CapitalOne360 (http://capitalone360.com): $0 to open an online checking or savings account (links to Capital One's **Sharebuilder** at **http://sharebuilder.com** for brokerage)

TDAmeritrade (http://tdameritrade.com): $0 to open a brokerage account ($2,000 to open a margin account)

Charles Schwab (http://www.schwab.com): $0 to open Hi-Yield Checking, $1,000 to open brokerage account

Fidelity (http://www.fidelity.com): $0 to open Cash Management checking, $2,500 to open brokerage account

Scottrade (http://www.scottrade.com): $500 to open brokerage, checking available for brokerage customers

To check out other banking options online or locally, visit **Bankrate.com**. The site can also help you find great rates, loan calculators, debt and retirement calculators - it's a great all-around resource.

Once you've chosen an account, to use it as your base account means this is the primary account where you deposit money set aside for investing. Look at this example.

Let's say you've been putting away $10 a week into your base account. Occasionally you bump up the amount to $25 or $50. In about two months, you'll have saved up $100. Now that you have at least $100, you can consider moving that money into a certificate of deposit, or a low-cost mutual fund or ETF (more on these later). You'll only move your money out of your base account if you find something that earns you a better rate, interest, or a dividend.

Congratulations - you've already gotten through step two of the three-step plan!

Chapter 3: When NOT to Pay Off Debt!

One common question from investors just starting out is what to do first: pay down debt, or set money aside to start investing. This is truly a "chicken and egg" question. When you don't have a lot of extra cash coming in, yet you want to save for multiple purposes, it's hard to decide where to put your resources.

You can find knowledgeable investment advisors on both sides of the argument. Some advisers will give you a good reason why you should pay down debt first – why save money when you are paying interest to creditors? Yet others will tell you to invest first, since you should build a cash cushion which you'll need in case of emergencies, and paying off debt means your cash is going to your creditors.

Both sides have good points to make. When you are weighed down by hundreds or thousands of dollars of credit card debt and loans at high interest rates, you're paying a lot of interest to the lender - and that's money goes straight into the bank's pocket, not yours. You are always out of pocket, and it's harder to save. Why save money in an account at 5% interest while you are also paying off a credit card balance at 22% interest? It just doesn't make sense! Any earnings from the one account is gobbled up by the interest on the other.

But what if you have a low interest rate on your debt? Or your minimum payments each month are reasonable, and you know you'll pay off everything in the near future? In that case, putting aside cash into an emergency fund may be more important than paying down debt so that you have money at hand. You should have an emergency fund of at least six months of your regular income. This is very important as a buffer against unforeseen economic events. Once your emergency fund is fully funded, you can use more money to pay off your credit cards or loans.

So, what should you do?

In reality, these two approaches shouldn't be mutually exclusive. You should pay off debt at the same time you start to invest. Start getting into the habit of setting aside even a small amount in a savings account, with an eye toward moving that lump into an investment account eventually. Contribute larger payments as you are able toward paying off debt. In the meantime, make sure you are making your monthly credit card payments on time, and put as much as you can into your investment account.

Get a second job if you have to, or liquidate some personal stuff on eBay or Craigslist. Do it today. Put that new money into your emergency fund, and build that up. Once you have a nice sum set aside, you can pay off debt. Once you have paid off one of your credit cards, for example, you can then deposit an amount equal to the monthly payment into your investment account. Now you're really paying yourself instead of your bank!

A lot of people wonder whether paying off their mortgage is a good idea, as well. This is the kind of debt you can hang onto at least for the short run. Your mortgage rate probably isn't high compared to other debt or potential rates of return. In addition, some of your interest is tax deductible, which is not true of credit card debt. If you are not delinquent on your loan, continue to make monthly payments on time, but don't worry about paying off your mortgage right away. It's more important that you build an investment base and emergency fund than it is to own your home free and clear. Once your investments are paying you in passive income, you can put those extra dollars toward paying down your mortgage loan.

So let's recap where you should be. So far, you've picked a specific amount of money you'll save each week and you have a plan for finding and saving that money (however small the amount) on a regular basis. You've decided to open (or have already opened!) a base account to accumulate your investment money. Finally, determine how much you'll allocate to debt, and how much to investing. Start putting at least small amounts into your base investing account.

Here are some resources to consider when deciding whether and how to pay off your debt:

Man vs. Debt (http://www.manvsdebt.com) – The subtitle tells it all: Sell Your Crap, Pay Off Your Debt, Do What You Love! Blogger Adam Baker tells exactly how he did just that and how you can too.

Dave Ramsey (http://daveramsey.com) – His books in the Total Money Makeover series and his Financial Peace program have helped hundreds of thousands of people get straightened out financially.

Suze Orman (http://suzeorman.com): Another financial industry all to herself, Suze has many resources to help viewers and readers learn how to respect money and put it in its proper place in their lives.

Now let's see where you can put your investment money once you've got it saved up.

Chapter 4: Why Savings Accounts Are "Risky"

Savings accounts have the reputation of being the "safest" of all investments. Your money is insured by the Federal Government, and you can withdraw it quickly if you need it. Many people consider savings accounts to be safer than other investment vehicles, like stocks, that are considered "risky". Yet keeping money in a savings account might actually be very risky; you could be losing more than you think. How do you know when or whether to stash money in the humble savings account?

Savings accounts are comparatively safe when it comes to your principal, that's certain. Deposits are protected under the Federal Deposit Insurance Corporation (FDIC), up to $250,000. This means that even if a bank fails, your deposits are protected and will be backed by the "full faith and credit" of the U.S. government for balances up to that amount. So you can be fairly sure that your principal is safe. And having demand access, meaning you can withdraw at any time, means you can get your hands on it right away. But that's where the benefits end. When it comes to making your money work for you, today's savings accounts fail miserably and can cost you in the end.

In past decades, keeping money in a savings account made sense. When interest rates were higher, at 5%, 7% or even more, savings accounts gave investors a decent return as well as safety. Today however, interest rates are extremely low, and almost at zero. For example, a survey of some national rates as of this writing (October 2012) shows many rates in the range of just 1% or less. To put that in perspective, that means that if you save $100, in the course of one year, you will earn $1 in interest. At that rate, you might be better off keeping your money under your mattress, where you can get it fast if you need it!

Today's low interest rates are the downside of savings accounts. Interest rates at 1% or below are likely to remain the norm for several years, based on the Federal Reserve's current policy of keeping rates down. That's a problem for investors in savings accounts, especially fixed income investors like retirees who want the safety of government backing, but are not earning enough interest to live on.

Worst of all, at these low interest rates, you may actually be losing money. The reason is that the rate of return on the account is lower than the rate of inflation. When inflation rises, prices rise and your money of today buys less than tomorrow. If your money is parked in an account where it is not matching the inflation rate, the buying power of your money is going down, and you are losing out.

As of publication dates, the inflation rate in the United States is about 2%. This means that every year, your cost of living goes up by 2%. So if you put your money into a savings account paying 1%, your money is not keeping up with inflation.

Consider what happens if you put $100 in a savings account paying 1% interest. You'll earn $1 on that $100 by the end of the year. However, at 2% inflation, your $100 when you withdraw it is now really just $98, so you've now *lost* $1.00 in buying power! You'd be better off buying lots of canned goods and storing them in the pantry - their value will rise faster than the money in your savings account. You can see why keeping money in low interest savings accounts is actually very risky, possibly even riskier than investing in the market, when you think about the loss of your buying power.

To add insult to injury, savers pay taxes on the interest their account earns. Savings interest is taxed as ordinary income, unlike (for example) capital gains from stock sales, which are taxed at a lower rate.

With small dollar investing, you probably won't make so much in interest that you'll have to worry about a huge tax hit. But consider that you've already lost 1% in buying power, and you're going to be taxed on the $1 you earned, losing 20-30% of that dollar, so on your $100 investment, over one year you really only earned 75 cents! These are important things to consider when deciding whether to keep money in a savings account.

Savings accounts are not the only safe option for protecting your money. If safety of your investment is part of your financial planning, consider savings accounts, but also U.S. Treasury Bonds, which have slightly better rates. In particular, take a look at the I Bond, which fluctuates with inflation. (See Chapter 6 for more on U.S. savings bonds.)

Despite these drawbacks, here are some good reasons why you *would* want to keep your money in a savings account:

- You need access to your cash in the short term, say six to twelve months. It's easy to get money out of a savings account fast if you need it (this could also be a bad thing, if you're trying to avoid spending this cash!).
- You're saving in a Christmas club account or other account for a specific short term purchase.
- You are teaching a child how to save money. Going to the local bank to deposit money can be fun, especially with an old-fashioned passbook account.
- You have plenty of money invested elsewhere, and want to keep some readily available for quick access and emergencies, or as a way to diversify your portfolio.
- You are receiving a higher rate of interest because you keep larger balances among several accounts.

For medium to long-term investing however, where your financial plan depends on receiving a decent return on your investments, a savings account probably isn't the most profitable choice. When the top rates that banks can offer are just 1%, you should explore different options that will help you achieve a better financial result. The best plan is to use a savings account as your base account to collect your small deposit amounts, and then, once you build up a larger account balance, transfer funds into investments with better return. You can choose other options such as money market accounts, stocks, bonds, and more, as you'll learn in the next few chapters.

You can find lists of current local and national savings account rates online at these websites:

Bankrate.com (http://bankrate.com): Website listing nation and local savings rates, along with CDs, loans and more.

MSN Money Savings Site (http://money.msn.com/budgeting-savings/: Ideas for budgeting and saving.

Yahoo! Finance Saving and Spending (http://finance.yahoo.com/saving-spending/): Yahoo! Finance has many saving and investing ideas.

Bankaholic (http://www.bankacholic.com/money-market): Lists money market rates nationwide.

Chapter 5: CDs: Not Much Better Than Savings Accounts

Certificates of deposit, usually shortened to just "CDs", are another very safe investment vehicle. Here's a definition of CDs from the website **InvestorWords.com**: "Short- or medium-term, interest-bearing, FDIC-insured debt instrument offered by banks and savings and loans." The idea behind CDs is that these instruments offer higher interest rates than most savings accounts, in exchange for the investor being willing to tie up their money for a certain time period, which is the CD's maturity date. CDs are considered low risk, and are usually insured similar to your deposits in savings accounts. Unfortunately, they have the same problems as savings accounts these days – extremely low returns which struggle to keep pace with inflation. Yet as with savings accounts, CDs might be a good investment under certain circumstances.

You can purchase a CD from a banking institution, usually for a fixed amount, such as $100, and for a fixed term anywhere from 3 months to six years. You can usually opt to either receive your interest payments quarterly during the term of the CD, or wait to be paid all of it at once, at the end of the term.

Usually, the longer the term of the CD, the higher the interest rate (although again, in the current economic climate, rates are still very low). When the CD's term expires, you receive back your principal investment and remaining interest payments. That's it. You can also choose to "roll over", or reinvest, the CD and interest into a new CD, which again ties up your money for a fixed length of time. Continually rolling over your CDs is called "laddering" similar to what investors do with bonds.

The interest rates paid (as of publication date) on CDs are close to those on savings accounts, that is, very, very low. An example of current rates from one financial institution shows how low they are: rates are .65% for a 3 month, $1,500 CD, or a whopping 1.5% three year, $1,500. Earning only 1.5% over three years is almost ridiculous if you consider that you will pay a penalty for early withdrawal if you need the money.

As with savings accounts, any money you earn on a CD is taxable income. But also remember the impact that inflation will have on your CD investment – at these rates, CDs are not keeping up with inflation either. Until interest rates climb, a CD is not a very good place to invest if you're trying to significantly grow your money.

CDs might make sense if you're simply looking for a way to keep the money out of your hands so it doesn't get spent. But be aware that there are at least four or five other places you can also stash your money safely and earn a better return.

Some reasons to buy CDs are:

- You are planning to give the CD as a gift, similar to a savings bond.
- You want to keep the money rolling over in fixed amounts for a fixed time period at a set interest rate, much like bonds.
- You need an investment vehicle to safely stash your savings so you can't easily cash it in and spend it.
- You want a secure investment for money you'll need in the next 1 to 3 years.

You can find lists of current CD rates at banks across the country at the following websites:

Bankrate.com (http://bankrate.com): National and local rates for CDs and money market funds

Bankaholic (http://bankaholic.com): CD rates from banks nationally and locally

Chapter 6: Old Faithful: U.S. Savings Bonds (And Other Bonds)

As a child, did you ever receive a savings bond as a gift? The U.S. Savings Bond is familiar to many as a way to safely save for the future, by investing in the United States. The U.S. has long been considered the strongest and safest place to invest worldwide for decades, and that is why the savings bond has been such a central part of the American financial fabric.

First, let's define what a bond is, since this can be confusing to new investors. Essentially, a bond is a loan of money by the person purchasing the bond made to the party who issues the bond. A bond in its simplest terms is an agreement to repay you for your loan. A rate of interest is set for the loan, as well as a term for paying off the loan. Bonds are often used by investors as a way to diversify a portfolio, since bonds generally tend to rise and fall in value opposite the stock market. That is, when stocks are doing poorly, often bonds are doing better, and vice versa. U.S. Savings bonds are the easiest way for U.S. citizens to "invest" in the U.S. Government. When politicians talk about "the debt", they mean money the Government owes on Treasury loans to investors including holders of savings bonds. U.S. bonds were also popular in times of war, to help raise needed funds to support World War II for example, when it became absolutely patriotic to buy bonds.

Today, the digital age has changed the way people can buy U.S. Savings Bonds. The days of ordering a paper bond at the bank are now gone, giving way to electronic purchasing. As of January 2012, you can no longer purchase a paper bond from a financial institution (although you can order I Bonds from the IRS with your tax refund). To purchase savings bonds today, the U.S. Treasury has set up an online marketplace, called Treasury Direct.

At **TreasuryDirect.gov**, it's easy purchase a wide variety of investments from the Federal Government. Many of these investments such as T-bills and Treasury notes were once available only through an authorized broker, but now buyers can purchase online. You can own U.S. Savings Bonds if you have a Social Security Number and you're a:

- Resident of the United States.

- Citizen of the United States living abroad (must have U.S. address of record).

- Civilian employee of the United States regardless of residence.

- Minor. Unlike other securities, minors may own U.S. Savings Bonds.

For new investors with smaller amounts to invest, purchasing instruments from TreasuryDirect can be a good way to start making your money work for you, as well as putting part of your investing on autopilot.

One plus of U.S. bonds is that they're very safe investments, since they are backed by the U.S. Government. Some of the bonds do provide rates of return that are better than those you can get in a regular savings account. Bonds are easy to purchase online by using withdrawals from your designated bank account, direct deposit from your paycheck, or even automated regular purchases. You can also set up accounts for minor children. TreasuryDirect now also allows you to deposit money into a zero-interest account from which you can buy bonds later, by using direct deposit set up from your employer or scheduling a regular transfer from your personal checking or savings account.

What make these bonds so appealing for small dollar investors is the low startup cost. You can purchase an I bond or an E Bond with just $25, with direct withdrawals from your personal checking account or from an account you fund with the Treasury (called the "Zero Percent C of I" account). There is no fee or commission for purchasing savings bonds.

The downside of U.S. savings bonds is that your money is not quickly accessible. There is paperwork which must be completed to withdraw, and there also may be a penalty (in the form of reduced interest) if you withdraw too soon after purchase. As with other savings-type account, the interest you earn on bonds is also taxable, with some exceptions if the funds are used for retirement or education expenses.

To buy U.S. bonds, you need to set up a Treasury Direct account online. Link this account to your chosen bank account, such as your base account. You can then buy bonds directly via a debit transfer from your bank, or deposit money into your zero account at the Treasury to purchase later.

A variety of investments are available, including I bonds, EE Bonds, TIPS, T-bills and Treasury notes. There is extensive information available at the **TreasuryDirect** site to explain what all of these investments are, and how to purchase them.

For beginning and small dollar investors, however, the I bond and the EE bond are the best way to start out. For EE bonds, these are sold at face value; i.e., you pay $50 for a $50 bond, in amounts of $25 or more, to the penny. There is a $10,000 maximum purchase in one calendar year, and the bonds are issued electronically to your designated account.

EE bonds work the way they have worked for decades - you purchase a bond at 100% of its face value with a fixed interest rate. The bond accrues over time until you can cash in the bond for double its value at 20 years. You can wait even longer, since the bond continues to accrue at the fixed rate of interest for up to 30 years. If you redeem EE Bonds in the first 5 years, you'll forfeit the 3 most-recent months' interest. If you redeem them after 5 years, you won't be penalized.

Being able to purchase bonds in increments of $25 make these bonds very accessible to the small investor. Some investors don't like to invest in the EE bond, since the fixed rate of interest doesn't take advantage of fluctuating interest rates over time. As a result, you lose out when interest rates are higher. For these investors, the Treasury released the I Bond. The interest rate paid on the I bond fluctuates with the rate of inflation (for details about how this is calculated, visit the TreasuryDirect website.) This means that the money invested will at least match the rate of inflation, and not stay stagnant at a fixed rate if interest rates rise.

As with EE bonds, I bonds are sold at face value; you pay $50 for a $50 bond. They must be purchased in amounts of $25 or more, to the penny, with a $10,000 maximum purchase in one calendar year. Bonds are issued electronically to your designated account. If you want to purchase a paper I bond, these are only available through your IRS tax refund, and you receive a paper bond certificate. They are also sold at face value; i.e., you pay $50 for a $50 bond, and must be purchased in denominations of $50, $75, $100, $200, $500, $1,000, and $5,000. You can purchase a $5,000 maximum purchase in one calendar year.

If you redeem I Bonds within the first 5 years, you'll forfeit the 3 most recent months' interest; after 5 years, you won't be penalized. Also, for both the I and the EE bonds, you must hold the bond for 12 months before redeeming it, and after 30 years, the interest stops accruing.

Your bonds can be easily redeemed online, with the proceeds then deposited into the bank account you have attached to your Treasury Direct account. This process takes a few days to clear into your bank account.

U.S. Savings bonds aren't the only kind of bonds on the market. Since issuing bonds is simply a way of raising money from investors, all kinds of institutions, such as governments, utilities and corporations, offer bonds. Bonds you can purchase from a broker include corporate bonds (loans to corporations), municipal bonds (loans to municipalities for capital expenditures), and utility bonds (loans to utilities for capital purposes).

Municipal and some utility bonds can be tax free if you live in the municipality whose bonds you are purchasing, which means you don't pay state taxes on the interest payments you receive. This can boost the actual rate of return of a bond compared to other vehicles whose dividends or interest is taxable (like stocks or savings accounts). Check with your broker to find out if the bonds are tax advantaged for you.

When buying corporate or government bonds through your broker, minimum purchases apply, and often that means you'll need at least several thousand dollars. For small investors, this can be prohibitive. Instead of buying bonds directly, you instead have the option of buying a bond ETF, or a bond mutual fund. These funds invest in a basket of bond holdings and can be a much less expensive way to take advantage of diversifying your portfolio by holding bonds. Read more about mutual funds and ETFs in Chapters 7 and 8.

Check online for the current Treasury rates for savings and other bonds. You might find the rate is higher than your savings account, and for money you don't need right away, these can be an excellent investment. Once you have larger amounts of money to invest, you may want to consider holding Treasury notes and bills for safe, higher interest rates, as well as some corporate or municipal bonds.

You can learn more about investing in bonds with these resources:

TreasuryDirect.gov – The U.S. Treasury website for purchasing Treasury bonds

Investing In Bonds from the Bond Market Association – http://investinginbonds.com

CNN Money Bond Basics - http://money.cnn.com/magazines/moneymag/money101/lesson7/index.htm

SmartMoney Magazine Bond Investing - http://www.smartmoney.com/invest/bonds/

Chapter 7: Should You Avoid Investing In Mutual Funds?

If you have a 401(K) retirement account today, or had money in the market in the last decade, you've probably had shares in a mutual fund. In the decades before the 2008 market downturn, many small and novice investors were told to invest in mutual funds as an easy way to participate in the stock market. Mutual funds were also touted as a simple way to "diversify", or avoid having all of your money invested in just one or two vehicles.

Mutual funds are investment vehicles set up to purchase a variety of investments, usually stocks. Members invest money, and are given proportional shares of the fund- you never personally hold any given stock or stocks. The manager of the fund then buys stocks, and the profits, losses and tax consequences are shared by all purchasers of shares in the fund. A huge variety of fund choices is available, covering virtually every type of investment vehicle and combination of stocks, fund with fees and funds without fees, funds with small initial deposits, and funds with larger initial deposits.

However, there are drawbacks of mutual funds for small investors that you might not know about. How mutual funds work is different from simply buying a stock or ETF. It's important to know more about the inner workings to avoid the pitfalls of investing in mutual funds.

Mutual funds are essentially a basket of stocks. This means the fund holds shares in a variety of investments. As noted above, you, the investor, simply buy shares of the mutual fund, not shares of the component stocks or investments.

There are several issues to keep in mind when investing in mutual funds. First and foremost, you don't get to choose what investments the fund holds.

For example, if you invest in an "international fund", the fund might hold 85% of its investments in European stocks, with only 15% from other international locations. As another example, an index fund will hold stocks in a particular index, regardless of how badly the index might be performing.

Another problem with mutual funds is timing. Mutual fund purchases and sales take place only at the end of the market day, after the stock traders have had their way with the market. This is unlike stocks or ETFs, where you, the investor, can sell shares immediately in the market at any time during the trading day. Mutual fund investors get the last price of the day – which as we saw in 2009, may, in some cases, be too late to avoid downturns in the market. Timing was one reason why many investors lost money during large daily market moves during the economic crash.

The attraction of mutual funds for small investors was that it has been historically sold as a way to be in the market without having to know how to trade single stocks - you only had to buy the funds and hold until you retire. This is a dangerous assumption however. To be fair, mutual funds make the standard disclaimer they are required to make by law, that you should be an informed investor before investing in the market. However there has also been plenty of misinformation from so-called financial advisers and gurus, which has gone undisputed by the mutual fund industry, that buying "good" mutual funds and "holding for the long run" is the best way to succeed if you don't know anything about investing.

Nothing could be further from the truth. During the crash of 2008-2009, small investors had a gut feeling they should get out, but were told – by television finance journalists and other self-proclaimed experts - to maintain their "buy and hold" strategy and not panic. Meanwhile, professional investors pulled out of investments to hold cash while the storm passed. Small mutual fund investors got the worst of the advice and market timing.

Unfortunately, mutual funds continue to be sold to beginning investors by touting them as an easy way to diversify or a good place to park money and reap big benefits later. That's no longer true, and today investors need to pay attention to their investments more closely. Despite the downsides, mutual funds remain the primary investment of choice for corporate 401(k) retirement accounts and are often the only option employees have. This isn't a surprise: many 401(k) plans are administered by big mutual fund companies! Funds are often conservative because employers don't want the responsibility of having employees lose money, even though that can happen anyway during big market moves.

Another problem with mutual funds is associated costs. Between fees and charges, called the "load", some investors pay as much as 5% or even more to purchase shares of a mutual fun. No-load funds are available, but even these often have management fees and tax consequences. And while some fund companies don't charge fees, an initial deposit of several thousand dollars can be a barrier to the beginning or small investor. There can also be capital gains owed. When a fund manager buys and sells stocks that make up the fund, the investors owe the taxes on capital gains. This can add up to costs even if you haven't taken your investment out of the fund.

Something else that is often overlooked by small investors in mutual funds is knowing what specific investments are held in their chosen funds. Investors who aren't reading the fine print in the fund prospectus might not be aware of what exactly they are investing in.

For example, some international funds have a majority European exposure – which was problematic during Europe's economic downturn - and very little Asian exposure - where more profit is being made. Often, mutual fund investors are told to just buy an index fund, supposedly an easy way to diversify - yet indexes can still be heavily weighted in a specific industry. For example, the S&P 500 includes a significant portion of financial companies, which took a big hit in the economic crash of 2008.

When considering mutual funds as an investment, make sure you understand clearly the risks and costs of these investments. Make sure they are a good fit with your investment needs. It is clear that you should never put your money in a mutual fund or any other investment unless you know how the market works. Know when you want to buy and under what conditions you will sell your holdings, to protect your principal and make the best profit possible. With the huge number of excellent educational resources available today, there is no excuse for not taking time to learn about investing *before* you invest!

Remember to ask yourself, "Is this the best use of my money?" and "Am I getting the best return I can for this investment?" Maintain your control over your own brokerage account, as well as over rollover retirement accounts, including the specifics of any investments held by your mutual fund investments.

Today, you have lower cost, less risky alternatives to mutual funds. You might explore investing in Exchange Traded Funds (ETFs). These are funds made up of baskets of stocks, commodities and other investments, which trade just like individual stocks and without the high fees and restrictions of mutual funds. You'll read more about them in Chapter 10.

As another alternative, you may do better than mutual funds by purchasing individual stocks, ETFs, or even bonds, if you are willing to learn how to invest your money. Until you have built a bigger portfolio, and have taken the time to calculate the actual costs of owning mutual funds, you may want to avoid mutual funds in favor of ETFs and other investment vehicles, or just hold cash until you have a solid investment plan in place.

That said, if you feel comfortable with mutual funds, just make sure you do your research into the holdings and costs of the funds you're interested in. Search out the low cost funds, and those with small initial investments. Avoid index mutual funds and instead buy index ETFs. Finally, only choose funds with a portfolio that specifically provides a type of investment you want. Whether that is large cap stocks, small caps stocks, Asian investments and so on will depend on your research, your financial plan and what you've determined you need to be properly diversified and achieve the returns you seek.

You can find more information about mutual funds at the websites noted below. Mutual fund research is available from nearly all brokerage companies - just check your company's website.

Motley Fool: **http://www.fool.com**

Morningstar Mutual Fund Ratings: **http://www.morningstar.com**

Chapter 8: Why ETFs Can Be Better Than Mutual Funds

One type of investment vehicle is growing by leaps and bounds due to its ease of use and flexibility: exchange traded funds, known as ETFs. These funds are similar to mutual funds only in that they are essentially baskets of stocks which mimic stock market indexes, or baskets of commodities or bonds or other investments.

The similarity with mutual funds pretty much ends there. With ETFs, you buy single shares of ETFs in the same way you buy individual stocks, purchasing a number of shares at a market (or limit) price during regular stock market hours. Unlike mutual funds, which trade only at the close of the market and are bought in dollar amounts rather than number of shares, you can buy and sell ETFs for the price you choose throughout the trading session.

What makes ETFs so appealing for all investors is that you can own ETF shares in a huge variety of investment vehicles, at a price per share, with no minimum investment. This allows even small investors to buy groups of stocks, bonds or even commodities in reasonably priced amounts. For example, you can buy an ETF that combines the S&P 500 stocks for around $100 a share. That's much easier than investing in shares of a mutual fund, which may have minimum investment amounts of as much as $3,000 or $5,000, plus management and other fees.

Buying ETFs is also easier than buying several hundred individual stocks on your own. An ETF can aggregate stocks in certain industries, stock indexes, or countries. You can buy bond ETFs that invest in corporate bonds, Treasury bonds, and foreign bond issues.

You can buy agriculture ETFs that invest in corn, soy or wheat. Or, get in on the precious metals bandwagon by purchasing ETFs comprised of gold stocks, silver, or other precious metals without having to buy the metals themselves. The variety of ETFs, like mutual funds, is seemingly endless.

As with mutual funds, ETFs also have management fees and other costs that are built into the price. You should review the prospectus for an ETF just as you would a mutual fund prior to investing.

So how do you start investing in ETFs? As with stocks, you buy them through a brokerage account. If you have been following along from the beginning of this book, you should already have a brokerage account open. Start with your broker to research ETFs available to trade, their prices, holdings, and other information. Check to see if your broker offers any ETFs commission free, which will save you even more money. As with mutual funds, be sure you read the prospectus and learn what actual investments the ETF holds. Also, note that some brokers, notably Sharebuilder, limit what ETFs you can purchase. As with any investment, make sure you do you research and review your financial plan before you jump into buying ETFs.

As a very basic starting point, here are some ETFs to research. Look up the symbol just like a stock symbol:

SPDR Dow Jones Industrial Average: symbol DIA

SPDR S&P 500 Index: symbol SPY

PowerShares QQQ Trust (NASDAQ index): symbol QQQ

iShares Russell 2000 Index: symbol IWM

iShares Gold: symbol GLD

PowerShares DB Bullish US Dollar: symbol UUP

iShares Barclays 20+ Year Treasury Bond: symbol TLT

PowerShares DB Oil Fund: symbol DBO

You can find ETFs for virtually any investment. For a good online searchable directory of all ETFs, visit the **Stock Encyclopedia ETF List: http://etf.stock-encyclopedia.com/.**

Learn more about ETF investing at **The Motley Fool ETF Investing in 60 Seconds: http://www.fool.com/investing/etf/index.aspx**

Chapter 9: Cheap Commissions Means More $$ For You

For small dollar investors, keeping your investing costs to a minimum is imperative. The higher your commission fees or other costs, the more money is taken out of your pocket, and less money is working for you. To make sure that the maximum amount possible is going into your investment portfolio, pay attention to the fees and costs of any investment you purchase.

The main fee you'll pay for investing is the commission charged by your broker to buy stocks or ETFs and other investments. Online discount brokers were invented to allow investors to pay very low fees by making their own investment purchases online. Internet brokers offer fees anywhere from $4.95 to $19.99 per trade, with most in the ballpark of $10 per trade.

When you are only buying smaller amounts, you have to consider the cost of commissions as it compares to your investment amount. For example, if you pay $9.99 per trade, and you're only investing $100, that trade is costing you 10% of your principal to buy that investment. Just to break even, your investment will have to earn at least 10%, a return that is very aggressive. Rather than be in hole 10% right off the bat, wait until you have more money to invest, or use a lower cost broker. Remember too, that when you sell you will pay the same commission, which means that, for that $100 stock buy, your stock investment will have to have grown by 20% just for you to break even.

Here's a real world example. Say you have $100 to invest, and your broker charges $10 per trade. You buy ABC Stock at a share price of $75, so your entire cost is $85. Say ABC Stock increases to $90 per share, and you decide to take your profit – except that you'll pay another $10 in commissions to sell.

In this scenario, your account has actually lost money – because you paid a total of $95 to get in and out of the stock - $75 plus $20 in fees. Instead, say you invest $750 to buy ten shares and the stock goes up to $95 per share. Your investment has increased $200, and if you sell, you'll deduct your purchase amount of $750 plus $20 in fees to buy and sell, leaving you with $180 profit. You can see that it doesn't pay to buy stocks until you have enough to pay the fees involved.

Paying the high fees is one reason many small investors go broke in the market, because they simply don't take the costs into account. Remember: every dollar you pay in commission is a dollar that is NOT going into your own pocket! Whether you're investing for retirement, college or just a rainy day, your portfolio will grow faster when you pay lower fees. You'll be saving more of your hard-earned dollars toward your goal, and not spending them on fees and costs.

The best way to keep your costs low is to use discount brokers that charge between $5 and $10 per trade. Several reputable online brokers now offer low fees like this. Here are some of the top discount brokers and the fees they are charging as of June, 2013:

TradeKing (http//tradeking.com): $4.95

Sharebuilder (http://sharebuilder.com): $4.00-$6.95

Scottrade (http://www.scottrade.com): $7.00

Fidelity (http://www.fidelity.com): $7.95

TDAmeritrade (http://tdameritrade.com): $9.99

Charles Schwab (http://www.schwab.com): $8.95

One of these brokers operates a little differently from the others. Sharebuilder, now owned by the credit bank giant Capital One, is a great place for beginning investors to get started. The idea behind Sharebuilder is to help investors get in the habit of investing money on a regular basis. Part of this means the costs need to stay very low. Sharebuilder helps you put your investing on autopilot, so that deposits and stock purchases can be scheduled automatically.

If you invest regularly, paying fees constantly will eat away at your earnings. Sharebuilder offers a low $4 commission on scheduled purchases, but you can reduce that even more if you invest frequently. For frequent investors, there is a plan that charges $12 per month to make six trades per month. For anyone using direct deposit to invest each paycheck, this is a great way to slash your commissions. (To sell a stock, or to buy at market, as you would at another broker, the commission is $9.99.)

Another benefit of Sharebuilder is that it allows investors to buy what is known as "fractional shares." Nearly all brokers will require you to buy in full share increments when you make a purchase. At Sharebuilder, however, you can buy a certain dollar amount, regardless of how many shares that will buy. For example, you can purchase $25 worth of a $50 stock, which means you will own half a share. This is important if you are investing a specific dollar amount an a periodic basis, such as weekly or bi-weekly, you no longer have to worry about how many shares that will buy.

Many discount brokers now also offer additional commission savings by offering trades of certain ETFs or other products commission-free. But let the buyer beware: a commission of $0 isn't a good reason by itself to buy! Be careful to analyze these investments and do your product research. If you decide that it's an investment you would buy even for a higher commission, then you're on the right track, and can save some cash by using these services.

Certain other discount brokers have also lowered their fees to come close to the $5 commission. For example, Charles Schwab and Fidelity offer commissions under $8 to compete with the super low discounters.

With all of these companies, there's a huge plus today: They all offer a massive amount of investor education resources. You can take advantage of research tools, video training, webinars, investing information, training, portfolio analysis tools and many other services. You can also find brokers that have free checking and debit cards. Customer service is usually excellent as well, but be wary of placing trades through an operator, as the commission is usually very high compared to online trades.

Spend some time researching the costs and services at different brokerage companies, and choose one that has low fees and low minimum initial investment to open. You can always upgrade as your portfolio grows. Be sure to check for additional fees and costs, such as the cost to maintain or close an IRA or ROTH account, or fees for overdrafts, telephone trading, and other services.

Once you've opened your account, you can set up an electronic transfer between your base account and your brokerage to start taking advantage of a wider variety of investments, and get your money working for you. Here again is a list of top ranked brokerage houses with the minimum to open an account:

TradeKing (http//tradeking.com): $0

Sharebuilder (http://sharebuilder.com): $0

Scottrade (http://www.scottrade.com): $500

TDAmeritrade (http://tdameritrade.com): $0

Charles Schwab (http://www.schwab.com): $1,000

Fidelity (http://www.fidelity.com): $2,500

You can find more broker comparisons at **The Motley Fool (http://www.fool.com)**, as well as an annual brokerage comparison from sites and magazines like **SmartMoney's annual survey of best and worst discount brokers: (http://www.smartmoney.com/invest/markets/smartmoneys-annual-broker-survey-23119/).**

Chapter 10: Buy Gold and Silver for Just Five Bucks - Really!

You hear a lot about investing in gold on television, in the news, even on street corners where those "We Buy Gold" stores are popping up. Gold prices have soared in the last five or ten years, and it's become one way some investors choose to hedge against economic downturns. For small investors, now more than ever before, access to investing in precious metals is easily available. Thanks to ETFs, you can invest not just in gold and silver, but other commodities as well.

The gold purchased by investors is gold bullion, which consists of gold metal stock minted into coins by governments around the world and sold as one ounce coins or a fraction of an ounce. (These are NOT the "collectables" sold on television.) Gold prices are high, at more than $1,200 for a mere 1 oz. bullion coin as of this publication date When you buy bullion, there are also high commissions and fees to take into account as part of your overall cost of purchase. However, many advisors suggest adding some gold or silver to your portfolio, up to 10%, to maintain diversity of investments. These precious metals will general go up in price when stocks go down, although prices can fluctuate with world events and also with currency flutuations.

As always, make sure you research whether this investment is right for you, as every investment is a personal decision based on your own investment strategy. If you decide to buy gold, the way to get in with small amounts is to purchase a gold or silver ETF. There are also ETFs for other precious metals. Here are a few you should take time to research and familiarize yourself with:

SPDR Gold Trust: symbol GLD

iShares Gold Trust: symbol IAU

iShares Silver Trust: symbol SLV

ProShares Ultra Silver: symbol AGQ

As noted above, though, since gold is around $1200 per ounce, this means that a 1/10-ounce coin will cost at least $120 or more with fees and charges. But buying single gold coins in this size isn't usually smart financially. Expect to pay a commission of anywhere from 10% to 25% for your purchase, or a flat minimum of $25 or so. Fees will depend on how much bullion you are buying, and can be high if you are only buying a small amount. However, just as with stocks, commissions take up less of your total cost when you invest larger amounts. As with stock commissions, don't throw your money away by paying very high fees to own just a little bit of gold.

Gold bullion is purchased through a dealer. To find a dealer, search online for "gold bullion" or "gold bullion dealer" in your zip code. (Note: You are NOT looking for the We Buy Gold shops!) You can also broaden your search by state, as some dealers will ship your purchase. Many local coin dealers in your neighborhood are also likely to sell bullion. If they are a small shop, though, prices can be high. Be sure you spend time contacting several dealers to compare prices, fees and commissions. This is also the way to sort out the rip-off dealers from the dependable dealers. A good dealer will have many different bullion options for purchase, will have no problem with you examining the coins at length, and may offer other resources such as the option to store your gold bullion in their location to keep it safe, or allowing you to buy in monthly automatic purchases. Prices and fees will be stated right up front by the legitimate dealers, where small, expensive dealers might simply hide the fee in the purchase price. Do your research to save money.

When buying bullion, you'll end up with the physical investment instead of just numbers in an account. You'll need a safe place to keep bullion, like a safety deposit box at your bank. Many gold dealers also offer storage for a fee. If you're accumulating significant quantities of gold or silver bullion, consider finding out more about these services. You may want to skip these services if having immediate access is important to you.

If you only have small amounts of cash yet want to own gold, buying ETFs is likely your best bet until you build more of a base, and then you can sell your ETFs and use the proceeds to buy bullion. In a gold ETF, the ETF fund is the physical holder of the gold bullion, and sells shares of ownership in its gold stock. The price of gold ETFs will roughly parallel the price of gold on the market: however you can avoid the expense of commissions, and the difficulty of storing the gold safely, by purchasing ETFs.

Gold isn't the only commodity you can own, either. Consider adding some silver to your portfolio, or even other commodities as such as agricultural ETFs, oil, or currencies. These are more volatile investments, so again, take time to learn about these alternatives, and do your research before investing. But the bottom line is that using ETFs allows you to invest in these products and investment vehicles with smaller investment amounts. This means you can better diversify your portfolio and be better prepared to withstand market shifts.

Chapter 11: Which Small Dollar Investments to Buy

If you've read this far, you must be excited about getting started with small dollar investing. By now you should have followed the first two steps completely, and hopefully you've been up some cash in your base account. Now the question is where to put the funds?

Here's a list of recommended investment ideas, grouped by how much they require to get started. These are ranked based on lowest commissions and safest investments, until you build your account balances high enough to start investing in stocks and other investment vehicles.

Investing With $5 to $25

1. Save your money in a savings or money market account.

2. Save your money in a Sharebuilder account or brokerage money market until your balance is sufficient to purchase investments.

3. Deposit into U.S. Treasury Zero account until your balance is sufficient to buy Treasury bonds.

Investing With $25 to $100

1. Save your money in a savings or money market account.

2. Save your money in a Sharebuilder account or brokerage money market until your balance is sufficient to purchase investments.

3. Deposit into U.S. Treasury Zero account until your balance is sufficient to buy Treasury bonds.

4. Buy A U.S. Treasury I Bond ($25).

5. Buy a CD for $100.

Investing With $100-$1000

1. Save your money in a savings or money market account.

2. Save your money in a Sharebuilder account or brokerage money market until your balance is sufficient to purchase investments.

3. Deposit into U.S. Treasury Zero account until your balance is sufficient to buy Treasury bonds.

4. Buy U.S. Treasury I Bonds ($25 increments)

5. Buy a CD for $100-$1,000.

6. Buy stocks or ETFs through a discount broker or Sharebuilder account (no-fee ETFs at your broker if available).

7. Buy no-load (i.e. no-fee) Mutual Funds with low minimum initial investments.

Investing With $1000-$5000

1. Save your money in a savings or money market account.

2. Save your money in a Sharebuilder account or brokerage money market until your balance is sufficient to purchase investments.

3. Deposit into U.S. Treasury Zero account until your balance is sufficient to buy Treasury bonds.

4. Buy U.S. Treasury I Bonds ($25 increments)

5. Buy a CD for $100-$1,000.

6. Buy more stocks or ETFs in your brokerage account.

7. Buy no-load (i.e. no-fee) Mutual Funds.

9. Begin to explore other investments such as commodities, options, currencies.

Investing With More Than $5,000

Once your account is greater than $5,000, you can invest in any or all of the above investment ideas, depending on your financial plan and the diversification that meets your needs. Keep a percentage of your money in cash-based accounts such as savings and money market, so that you can take advantage of "sales" when stocks drop. (As a guide, mMany advisers recommend keeping 10-30% in cash.) Given the volatility of the stock market, it's best not to put all of your investing dollars in the stock market basket!

Remember also that buying stock with less than $5,000 means your balances will be impacted by commissions, fees and price fluctuations. With balances smaller than $5,000, investing in stocks by buying fractional shares (such as with Sharebuilder) makes more sense because you will save on commissions. After your portfolio reaches higher balances, you'll have the opportunity to spread your risk a little more and try out some new investing strategies.

Once your account grows you can move into more sophisticated and varied investment vehicles. The way to achieve greater growth and profit is to learn about new options for investing. No matter what level of investor you are or become, never stop learning to invest! There are lots of tools to help you visualize new investments and how they work, such as the **Options Industry Council's free Virtual Trading System** (http://optionseducation.org). Some of the Resources listed in the next section can help you find new areas in which to profit.

Have fun, keep exploring, keep investing, and grow your wealth. You've started your investment journey: your job now is to continue saving and investing for a secure financial future for you and your family.

More Investing Ideas and Resources

If you found this book helpful, Susan Calhoun has written several helpful books for beginning investors, available on Amazon.com.

The Easy Way to Invest in Mutual Funds: A Beginner's Guide

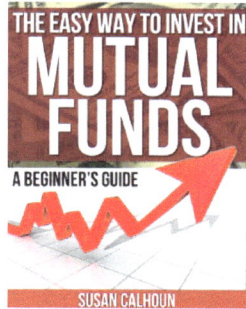

If you want to learn to buy precious metals, get a copy of:

The Easy Way to Invest in Gold: Precious Metals for the Beginning Investor

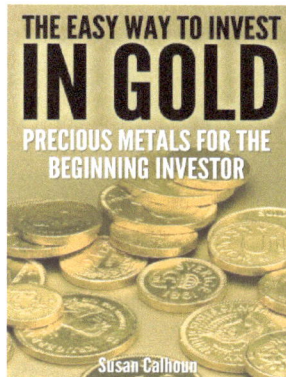

For retirement wealth ideas, get a copy of:

Boost Your 401(K): The Easy Way To Retirement Riches

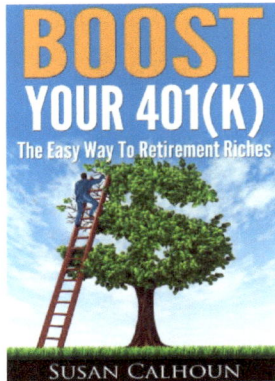

Visit **The Easy Way to Invest** blog for stock ideas, investing resources, along with new investing ideas, podcasts and video how-to at http://www.easywaytoinvest.com.

Get daily investing tips on Twitter:
http://twitter.com/easywaytoinvest

Your investment portfolio will be something you keep building and managing all of your life. It pays, literally, to keep learning what works and doesn't work in every economy you find yourself in. That's why keeping informed, and discovering new investing ideas, is the key to keeping your account growing.

The following resources can get you started, offering more ideas to learn about investing, find more investing ideas, and keep your knowledge, and as a result your portfolio, growing.

Books:

Investing for Dummies, by Eric Tyson. Easy to understand for all investors. The classic easy to use handbook of investing.

Investment Mistakes Even Smart Investors Make and How To Avoid Them, by Larry Swedroe and RC Balaban. Great for all investors, but small investors can profit if they avoid common mistakes.

Websites:

The Motley Fool (http://www.fool.com): Born in the heady days of the Internet bubble, there is still plenty of information especially for beginning investors.

Google Finance (http://google.com/finance): News and market quotes.

Yahoo! Finance (http://finance.yahoo.com): News and market quotes.

CNBC (http://cnbc.com): Website for the business cable channel. News and information.

SmartMoney Magazine (http://smartmoney.com): News and information on personal finance and investing.

Here's to your successful investing, and profitable returns!